LITTLE QUICK FIX:

KNOW YOUR NUMBERS

LITTLE
QUICK FIX:
KNOW YOUR NUMBERS

John
MacInnes

Los Angeles | London | New Delhi
Singapore | Washington DC | Melbourne

Los Angeles | London | New Delhi
Singapore | Washington DC | Melbourne

SAGE Publications Ltd
1 Oliver's Yard
55 City Road
London EC1Y 1SP

SAGE Publications Inc.
2455 Teller Road
Thousand Oaks, California 91320

SAGE Publications India Pvt Ltd
B 1/I 1 Mohan Cooperative Industrial Area
Mathura Road
New Delhi 110 044

SAGE Publications Asia-Pacific Pte Ltd
3 Church Street
#10-04 Samsung Hub
Singapore 049483

Editor: Mila Steele
Editorial assistant: Shelley de Jong
Production editor: Nicola Carrier
Copyeditor: Neville Hankins
Proofreader: Thea Watson
Marketing manager: Ben Griffin-Sherwood
Design: Shaun Mercier
Typeset by: C&M Digitals (P) Ltd, Chennai, India
Printed in the UK

Library of Congress Control Number: 2018945883

British Library Cataloguing in Publication data

A catalogue record for this book is available from
the British Library

ISBN 978-1-5264-5885-8 (pbk)

Contents

2 MIN
summary

Everything in this book!

Section 1 Numbers are important. Without practice, it's easy to get rusty with handling numbers. Being fluent with numbers makes all kinds of tasks easier. Numbers are basic to understanding many aspects of society, and with the data revolution taking place, they're more important now than ever.

Section 2 A fraction is the building block of a comparison. Fractions are the basic way of expressing proportions or parts of a whole number, usually between zero and one. Being able to describe and manipulate fractions of a number is the basis of making comparisons. Every fraction has a *numerator* and a *denominator*.

Section 3 Five interlocking rules tell you everything you need to know about dealing with fractions. Practise these rules and you'll have everything you need for using numbers to compare things.

Section 4 Learn to read a table. Tables convey massive amounts of information. The numbers in them allow us to make so many different kinds of comparisons, *all based on fractions*.

Section 5 We can compare things through a table's rows and columns. Numbers in the rows and columns of a table can be expressed in fractions. Comparing fractions based on rows along a column, or fractions based on columns along a row, tells us two different but equally powerful stories.

Section 6 Superfluous numbers are like fog. They make it harder to see clearly any message in the numbers. Three numbers are usually plenty. Get rid of the fog of numbers by *rounding*.

Section 7 Percentages and ratios help. Instead of just making comparisons, we often want to put a number on a comparison. That number is also a fraction or ratio, often expressed as a percentage. Note that there are a couple of traps to avoid!

Section

1

Being fluent with numbers makes all kinds of tasks easier

Why do numbers matter?

summary

Everyone needs numbers
because numerical descriptions
of the world – data – are vital for
everyday life.

Numbers are vital

We need numbers to express the relative size or scale of different phenomena. This makes them essential for social science, or for any course of study. We would struggle to describe many aspects of society without using numbers. Statements like 'most people work' or 'there are few women CEOs' are often not precise enough to capture the relationships or processes we're interested in explaining. Thus, we need numbers.

Most of the numbers we need to use and management of them require only basic arithmetic. However, unless you're sufficiently fluent in this management, your attention will be diverted onto this instead of staying with the story we're using the numbers to tell.

Unfortunately our brains aren't well adapted for numbers. That's why they require some concentration in a way that, for example, the rules of language – which are every bit as complex – do not. Some practice is essential.

WHY WE NEED NUMBERS

The data revolution has made data central to almost every university subject and every professional career. Being fluent in handling numbers is a basic skill that proves enormously useful for dealing with data and all kinds of numerical evidence, not only at work but also in everyday life.

Most of the maths you need is basic arithmetic, but it's easy to become rusty if you don't keep using these skills. If you last studied maths at school a few years ago you'll find a refresher helpful. Otherwise, the focus of your attention on what it is you're studying gets diverted onto sorting out how to handle the maths. Instead of being a vehicle for learning, the numbers can become an obstacle.

HOW TO GET YOUR HEAD AROUND NUMBERS

The good news is that there are many online and offline resources to help you understand numbers. Even better news is that the calculator on your phone or a spreadsheet package on a computer will instantly perform any calculation you'll ever need. The bad news is that no calculator in the world will tell you *which* calculation it is that you need to make. To understand that you need some basic rules and *there's no substitute for practice* in learning them: it's the only way to make the 'rules' second nature so that you don't have to waste time thinking about them.

WHY NUMBERS NEED CONCENTRATION

We use numbers to express quantity and report measurements: to grasp the scale of something. In everyday life on the savannahs a hundred thousand years ago the range of scale humans evolved to deal with was small. Thus we have a good intuitive feel for simple numbers and quantities like 'a little', 'a lot', 'some', and, perhaps using our fingers, we can manipulate numbers up to 10 without much thought.

MATHS BUILT THE PYRAMIDS

Mathematics was the first form of logically rigorous thought to be developed as settled agriculture made civilization possible. In the time of the Pharaohs maths was used to work out the area of arable land or the amount of tax revenues. However, the scale and complexity of modern society, or the measurements produced by scientific research, demand numbers that are at once more precise and range from the unimaginably small to the gigantic. Maths is used to hunt for the Higgs boson particle or estimate the size of the Galaxy.

WHY
CONCENTRATION
TAKES EFFORT

Our brains have not evolved to be particularly good at maths. That's why dealing with numbers takes effort and a clear head. The beauty of simple maths is that it is pure logic – all the rules fit together perfectly. They are also cumulative – each rule builds on others. A good foundation in the elementary rules set out here makes any maths or calculations you encounter very much easier, by making much of the logic 'second nature' and freeing up your working memory to deal with the problem at hand instead of thinking about how the tools you're using to deal with it work.

DON'T KEEP EVERYTHING IN YOUR HEAD

This means two things. First, pen and paper are essential. Writing things down saves trying to remember everything which can get jumbled up or forgotten. Second, practice is even more essential. You can read all about how to ride a bike and yet still fall off when you try it. Only practice makes balancing and steering, starting and stopping 'second nature' rather than something you have to concentrate on. The time invested in practising the basics described here will pay enormous dividends and save large amounts of time later.

THE REWARDS OF NUMBERS

People who are competent with numbers also enjoy a better life. Numbers can be good for your wallet, since these people are in relatively short supply and command good salaries. As one of them you could almost pick the kind of career or job that you genuinely want. It also makes you a much more critical consumer of numbers in everyday life, whether working out the true value of supermarket offers or the quality of 'evidence' offered in newspapers or by politicians.

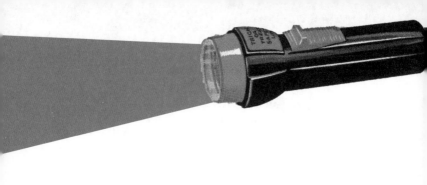

The data revolution also means that numbers are becoming steadily more important in almost every area of life. This does not require you to become a mathematical genius. You just need to be able to count and, just as important, to spot where numbers can be used effectively, or when they're being used well to illuminate, or badly to prop up, a poor argument. Most problems and challenges resolve into applying simple maths to complex situations, not complex maths to simple situations (which, unfortunately, tends to be the focus of most school maths).

I assume that you can add, subtract and multiply whole numbers? Let's make sure! Here's a quick quiz. Try it without a calculator if you can. If you get these questions right, you're good to go.

1 What is **136 + 59 + 11**?

2 From the list of numbers **7, 25, 32, 49, 55, 69, 80,** write down two numbers with a sum of **57**

3 A country has 25 million workers in its active workforce and 17 million people in its non-working population. What is the total population of this country?

4 What is **123,000 – 36**?

5 In one year, there was a total of **134,000** immigrants to a country, while 86,000 people left. What is the net migration into this country for that year?

6 What is **12 × 13**?

7 In the list of numbers **25, 32, 49, 55, 69, 86, 96**, circle all the multiples of 8

8 A researcher has **£2000** to pay respondents for a survey. If **125** people sign up for the survey, how much can the researcher pay each respondent?

9 A school board has **5** representatives per district council and there are 23 districts in the county. How many representatives are in the county?

1   206

2   25 + 32

3   42 million

4   122,964

5   48,000

6   156

7   32, 96

8   £16

9   115

You should've got all those right. If you need a quick refresher on the basics, there are online maths resources to suit all tastes. The following sites are worth trying if you need to check something:

www.mathsisfun.com

A US site covering years 1 through 12 of the school curriculum there.

www.mathtutor.ac.uk/

My favourite – very thorough but quite slow. There are both video and text versions of each topic.

www.khanacademy.org/math

Some people find Sal Khan's videos irritating, I find their obvious enthusiasm infectious.

Don't skip the exercises.
Practice _does_ make perfect.

23

A fraction is the building block of a comparison

Section

2

What's in a fraction?

A

Fractions have two numbers
and a line. The numerator is
the number above the line
and the denominator is the
one below the line.

60 SEC summary

Fractions represent parts of a whole, or proportions

Because we are often interested in comparing proportions in social science, fractions are one of its basic building blocks. If you want to compare the amount or type of work done by men and women or what they get paid for it; compare the views of different ethnic groups; or understand social, political or economic inequality, then you need to be able to handle fractions.

Fractions express values between zero and one. The denominator, or the bottom number, represents the whole amount divided into a number of equal parts. The numerator on top represents the part of that whole. It tells you how many equal parts of the whole you have. The value of a fraction is the numerator divided by the denominator.

Dividing the numerator of a fraction by its denominator converts it into a decimal. Multiplying a decimal by 100 turns it into a percentage.

Know your
NUMERATORS
FROM YOUR
DENOMINATORS

Most social science turns on comparisons of various kinds. We might want to compare how many children from different social class backgrounds get to university, or the proportion of people who think of themselves as religious, or whether men and women tend to enter different occupations. To make such comparisons we need *fractions, decimals and percentages.*

Fractions are formed when you divide a whole a number of times, or, essentially the same thing, cut it into a number of equal parts. You might eat a quarter of a pizza, spend one-third of your income on rent, or read about what 'one in ten adults' supposedly thinks about something. The number of *equal parts* would be four for quarters, three for thirds, ten for tenths, and so on. This provides the denominator for the fraction, which appears either underneath a horizontal line or to the right of a diagonal slash:

$$\frac{1}{4} \qquad 1/4 \qquad 1/4$$

$$\frac{1}{3} \qquad 1/3 \qquad 1/3$$

$$\frac{1}{10} \qquad 1/10 \qquad 1/10$$

Above the line or to the left of the slash we write the number of these parts or divisions in our fraction. This is the numerator of the fraction. In each of our first examples there was only one part so we have

$$\frac{1}{4} \qquad 1/4 \qquad 1/4$$

$$\frac{1}{3} \qquad 1/3 \qquad 1/3$$

$$\frac{1}{10} \qquad 1/10 \qquad 1/10$$

Of course, we can have any number of *equal parts* in the numerator. If you have eaten *three*-quarters of a pizza, left *two*-thirds of your chips uneaten and bought fast food for *four* out of your last ten meals, we would have

$$\frac{3}{4} \qquad {}^{3}/_{4} \qquad 3/4$$

$$\frac{2}{3} \qquad {}^{2}/_{3} \qquad 2/3$$

$$\frac{4}{10} \qquad {}^{4}/_{10} \qquad 4/10$$

You can also think of fractions as any whole number (the numerator) divided by any other whole number (the denominator).

An etymological trick to remember

You can remember these names by remembering that the denominator tells us the name of the fraction by describing the number of parts into which a whole number is to be divided (half, quarter, third, tenth, etc.), while the numerator specifies how many of those parts there are or the number of them (**one** half, **three** quarters, etc).

Look at the fractions below that are written in word form. Write the fractions in number form.

one-fifth **1/5**

four-eighths

three-twelfths

five-tenths

twenty-seven divided by thirty

five divided by one hundred

nine times out of every twenty

two out of five voters

every fourth woman

fifty-seven consumers
in every hundred

nine out of ten cats

ANSWERS

DO IT YOURSELF

1/5 4/8 3/12 5/10 27/30 5/100 9/20 2/5 1/4 57/100 9/10

HAVE I EATEN ALL THE PIZZA, OR A FRACTION OF THE PIZZA?

If the numerator is a smaller number than the denominator, we have a fraction whose value is less than one. If the numerator is a larger number, we have a number greater than one. If the numerator and denominator are equal, we have the number one. If I eat a whole pizza (four quarters) and then eat another half pizza, then I've eaten one and a half pizzas, or six quarters:

$$\frac{6}{4} = \frac{4}{4} + \frac{2}{4} = 1\frac{1}{2}.$$

FROM FRACTIONS TO DECIMALS

You can turn any fraction into a decimal number by dividing the numerator by the denominator using mental arithmetic, a calculator (your phone or computer will have one) or a spreadsheet package like Microsoft Excel. (If using Excel, just select any cell on a worksheet and enter an equals sign followed by the fraction, e.g. '=1/2', and press Enter.)

So, to convert 3/8 to a decimal, we calculate $3 \div 8 = 0.375$.

TURN YOUR FRACTIONS INTO DECIMALS

Now turn the fractions you wrote down earlier into decimal numbers.

Start with your fractions and, below each one, write down its equivalent as a decimal.

1/5 ....

4/8 ....

3/12 ....

5/10 ....

27/30 ....

5/100 ....

9/20 ....

2/5 ....

1/4 ....

57/100 ....

9/10 ....

Answers 0.2 0.5 0.25 0.5 0.9 0.05 0.45 0.4 0.25 0.57 0.9

FROM DECIMAL TO PERCENTAGE

You can turn any decimal into a percentage by multiplying by 100

A percentage is a convenient way of expressing a fraction. It is just a fraction with a denominator of 100. Since a decimal is really a fraction with a denominator of one, multiplying any decimal by 100 turns it into a percentage. 'Per cent' is just Latin for 'per hundred'. Each time that you shift the decimal point in a number one place to the right, you multiply it by ten. Shifting two places multiplies by 100 (10 × 10).

TURN YOUR DECIMALS INTO PERCENTAGES

DO IT YOURSELF

Turn the decimals you just produced into percentages

0.2 ....

0.5 ....

0.25 ....

0.5 ....

0.9 ....

0.05 ....

0.45 ....

0.4 ....

0.25 ....

0.57 ....

0.9 ....

Answers 20 50 25 50 90 5 45 40 25 57 90

40

YOU'RE ALL CAUGHT UP!

- ☐ FRACTIONS
- ☐ DECIMALS
- ☐ PERCENTAGES

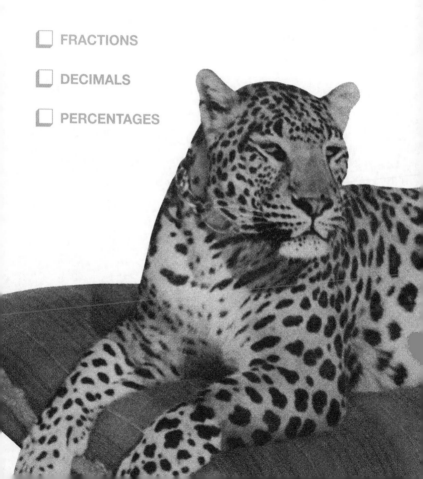

Got it?

Q: What are the two components of a fraction, and what does each of them mean?

Got it!

A: Denominator (on the bottom): the number of equal parts into which a whole is divided; Numerator (on the top): the number of those equal parts in the fraction

Got it?

Q: What is the value of
   a fraction?

Got it!

A: The numerator divided by the denominator

Five rules tell you everything you need to know about dealing with fractions

Section

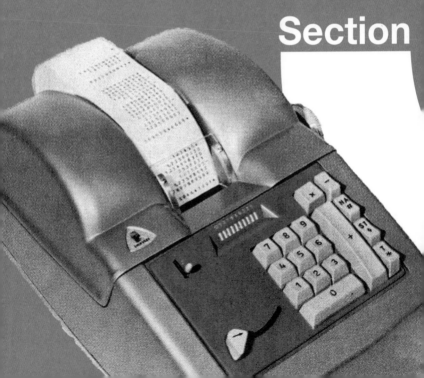

What are the five famous rules for fractions?

summary

Everything you need to know
about fractions boils down
to five rules. Each one leads
to the next.

summary

1 Dividing the numerator by the denominator gives the value of the fraction

2 Multiplying or dividing the numerator and denominator by the same amount leaves the value of a fraction unchanged

3 Any two (or more) fractions can be multiplied by taking the product of the numerators and product of the denominators. The denominators do not need to be the same number

4 To divide one fraction by another fraction, invert it and multiply

5 Adding and subtracting fractions requires the same denominator.

5 RULES DESCRIBE ALL THE CALCULATIONS YOU'LL EVER NEED TO MAKE WITH FRACTIONS

You don't need to memorize these rules. It's better to think through why they all must follow from how we define a fraction in the first place (rule 1)

Dividing the numerator by the denominator gives the value of the fraction

If I have half a pizza and cut it into three equal parts, I still have half a pizza but I just have more slices. Each of the three slices must now equal one-sixth of a pizza. So multiplying *both* parts of a fraction – the numerator and denominator – by the same amount doesn't change the value of the fraction, because *any number divided by itself must be equal to one.*

$$\frac{1}{2} = \frac{1}{2} \times 1$$

$$= \frac{1}{2} \times \frac{3}{3}$$

$$= \frac{1 \times 3}{2 \times 3}$$

$$= \frac{3}{6}.$$

If this is true for multiplying, it must also be true for dividing, so we arrive at our second rule

Multiplying or dividing the numerator and denominator by the *same amount* leaves the fraction unchanged:

$$\frac{2}{3} = \frac{2 \times 4}{3 \times 4} = \frac{8}{12} = \frac{800}{1200} = \frac{0.8}{1.2} = \frac{0.2}{0.3}.$$

If I have a quarter of a pizza and multiply that by 3, I must have three quarters! So if I multiply the numerator of a fraction by a whole number, then that must make the fraction bigger by a factor equal to that number:

$$\frac{1}{4} \times 3 = \frac{1}{4} \times \frac{3}{1} = \frac{3 \times 1}{4 \times 1} = \frac{3}{4}.$$

If I took each of my three quarters of pizza and divided them into three parts, I'd have nine slices, with each slice being one-twelfth. Dividing by three would leave me with 3/12 or 1/4 again. If I divide a fraction by a whole number, that must be the same as *multiplying* the *denominator* of the fraction by that number:

$$\frac{3}{4} \div 3 = \frac{9}{12} \div \frac{3}{1} = \frac{3}{12} = \frac{1}{4}.$$

$$\frac{3}{4} \div 3 = \frac{3}{3 \times 4} = \frac{3}{12} = \frac{1}{4}.$$

This gives us the third and fourth rules

. . . .

To multiply fractions we multiply the numerators together and then the denominators together. *It does not matter if the denominators are different*, you just multiply them:

$$\frac{2}{3} \times \frac{1}{4} = \frac{2 \times 1}{3 \times 4} = \frac{2}{12} = \frac{1}{6}.$$

. . . .

To *divide* a fraction by another whole number we *multiply* the denominator by that number:

$$\frac{2}{3} \div 4 = \frac{2}{3 \times 4} = \frac{2}{12} = \frac{1}{6}.$$

If the number we're dividing by (the divisor) is a fraction we invert that fraction and then multiply:

$$\frac{2}{3} \div \frac{1}{4} = \frac{2}{3} \times \frac{4}{1} = \frac{8}{3} = 2\frac{2}{3}.$$

To add or subtract fractions we first need to make the denominators the same. If I have one-third of a pizza and then help myself to another quarter, how much pizza do I have? I can't describe my new amount in either thirds or quarters. I have more than two quarters but less than two thirds. But if I think of my quarter of a pizza as three-twelfths, and my third of a pizza as four-twelfths, I now have seven-twelfths!

So the first and second rules must lead to the fifth rule

To add or subtract fractions they must *share the same denominator*, or have a *common denominator*:

$$\frac{1}{3} + \frac{1}{4} = \frac{4 \times 1}{4 \times 3} + \frac{3 \times 1}{3 \times 4}$$

$$= \frac{4}{12} + \frac{3}{12}$$

$$= \frac{3+4}{12}$$

$$= \frac{7}{12}.$$

$$\frac{1}{4} \times 3 = \frac{1}{4} \times \frac{3}{1} = \frac{3 \times 1}{4 \times 1} = \frac{3}{4}.$$

$$\frac{3}{4} \div 3 = \frac{3}{4} \times \frac{1}{3} = \frac{3 \times 1}{4 \times 3} = \frac{3}{12} = \frac{1}{4}.$$

#LittleQuickFix

To test your knowledge of the five famous rules, put a tick next to which of the following calculations you think are correct

$$\frac{2 \times 4}{3 \times 4} = \frac{2}{3} \times 4 = \frac{8}{3} = 2\frac{2}{3}.$$ ☐

$$\frac{2}{3} \div \frac{1}{4} = \frac{2}{12} = \frac{1}{6}.$$ ☐

$$\frac{2}{3} \div 4 = \frac{2 \times 4}{3} = 2\frac{2}{3}.$$ ☐

$$\frac{2}{3} \times \frac{1}{4} = \frac{2 \times 1}{3 \times 4} = \frac{2}{12} = \frac{1}{6}.$$

$$\frac{1}{3} + \frac{1}{4} = \frac{2}{7}.$$

$$\frac{1}{3} + \frac{1}{4} = \frac{4}{12} + \frac{3}{12} = \frac{4+3}{12}$$

$$= \frac{7}{12}.$$

$4/4 = 1$ not 4

$$\frac{2 \times 4}{3 \times 4} = \frac{2}{3} \times 4 = \frac{8}{3} = 2\frac{2}{3}.$$

to divide by 4 multiply
the denominator
$2 / 3 \times 4$

$$\frac{2}{3} \div 4 = \frac{2 \times 4}{3} = 2\frac{2}{3}.$$

to divide by 1/4 multiply
the numerator by 4
$2 \times 4 / 3$

$$\frac{2}{3} \div \frac{1}{4} = \frac{2}{12} = \frac{1}{6}.$$

before we add the
numerators together,
the denominators have to
be the same $1/3 = 4/12$
$1/4 = 3/12$

$$\frac{1}{3} + \frac{1}{4} = \frac{2}{7}.$$

The correct calculations are

$$\frac{2}{3} \times \frac{1}{4} = \frac{2 \times 1}{3 \times 4} = \frac{2}{12} = \frac{1}{6}.$$

$$\frac{1}{3} + \frac{1}{4} = \frac{4}{12} + \frac{3}{12} = \frac{4+3}{12} = \frac{7}{12}.$$

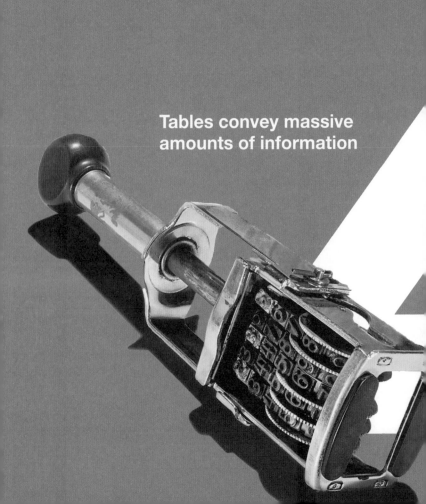

Tables convey massive
amounts of information

1 Section

How do
I make
sense of
tables?

10 SEC summary

The essence of tables is all the fractions that they display. To make comparisons easier, tables use decimals or percentages. They may or may not display the original numerators or denominators used to calculate them.

60 SEC summary

Tables help us compare things

Tables are a way of presenting many different fractions, and therefore many different comparisons, in one place. Remember that we can't add or subtract fractions with a different denominator (rule 5), so converting fractions in tables into decimals and percentages makes them easier to understand and work with.

We have already met decimals and percentages. Because they are so important in tables we look at how our number system works to understand them better.

Tables allow so many different comparisons to be made that you have to be clear about which comparisons you make when you read a table.

The way to learn about numbers is to dive right in and work with some actual numbers from the very beginning. Let's start by looking at a real table with real data. We'll use these numbers to practise working with decimals and percentages too. This table, from a Pew Research Center poll from August 2016, shows how people from different ethnic backgrounds said they would vote in a presidential election if Hillary Clinton and Donald Trump were the two candidates. In the survey, 1400 people took part.

	Clinton	Trump	Total
White	437	574	1011
Black	170	10	180
Hispanic	68	43	111
Other	57	41	98
All	732	668	1400

LOOKING AT ROWS AND COLUMNS

We might be interested in comparing the level of support for the two candidates in different ethnic groups. Each cell of the table shows the number of people in each ethnic group (displayed across the rows of the table) who said they would support each candidate (displayed in the columns). So, in this survey 437 White adults said they would vote for Clinton and 43 Hispanics said they would vote for Trump, and so on. The final column and the bottom row display the totals for the numbers in each column and row.

HOW DO WE FIND THE PATTERN IN THE NUMBERS?

How can we use these numbers to say something about how much support Clinton and Trump had in different ethnic groups? The trouble with the table as it stands is that any pattern in voting support is difficult to make out because there were different numbers of people in each ethnic category, and, of course, different total numbers expressing support for each candidate. How can we find the pattern?

We can use fractions, decimals and percentages to make the table clearer and see what messages it contains.

First let's examine the fraction of each ethnic group that supported Trump. This would give us the following fractions (rule 1):

White	574/1011
Black	10/180
Hispanic	43/111
Other	41/98
All	668/1400

Write in the fractions for each ethnic
group that supported Clinton

White ....

Black ....

Hispanic ....

Other ....

All ....

This doesn't take us much further, since we cannot readily compare
fractions with *different* denominators (rule 5). Is 43/111 larger or smaller
than 41/98? Unless you're a whizz at mental arithmetic, it's difficult to
say. To make them easier to compare, we can turn the fractions into
decimals, as we saw in Section 2. Let's look a little closer at decimals.

HOW DECIMALS WORK

We base our number system on the number 10 (probably because we have 10 fingers to count on). This means we write down numbers, reading from right to left in units, tens of units, tens times tens of units (hundreds), tens times tens times tens of units (thousands), and so on. So we write the number five thousand, two hundred and forty-three as 5243. It comprises the addition of five thousands, two hundreds, four tens and three units:

$$5243 = 5000 + 200 + 40 + 3$$

$$5 \times 1000 + 2 \times 100 + 4 \times 10 + 3 \times 1.$$

Decimals are a system to see and work with fractions of a whole number. We place a 'decimal point' after the units, and then write the number of tenths, hundredths, thousandths, and so on. Thus the whole numbers go to the left of the decimal point and the fraction to the right:

$$43.629 = 4 \times 10 + 3 \times 1 + 6 \times \frac{1}{10} + 2 \times \frac{1}{100} + 9 \times \frac{1}{1000}$$

$$= 4 \times 10 + 3 \times 1 + \frac{6}{10} + \frac{2}{100} + \frac{9}{1000}.$$

When we *multiply* a whole number by 10, 100 or any power of 10
we simply shift the decimal point to the right and put a zero in as a
'placeholder' if we need to:

43.209 × 10 = 432.09

43.209 × 1000 = 43,209

43.209 × 1,000,000 = 43,209,000

Equally, if we divide a number by a multiple of 10 we just shift the decimal point to the left, again inserting zeroes if need be:

$43.209 \div 10 = 4.3209$

$43.209 \div 100 = 0.43209$

$43.209 \div 1000 = 0.043209$

$43,209,000 \div 1,000,000 = 43.209$

Note that we don't need to keep trailing zeroes *after* the number to the right of the decimal point, or *before* the number to the left of the decimal point: 43.2090 is just 43.209, in the same way that 043.1 is the same as 43.1.

Remember too that each shift of place to the right in a number involves a 10-fold decrease in the value of a digit, just as each shift to the left involves a 10-fold increase.

Thus the number 0.095 is *smaller* than the number 0.12, in the same way as the number 120 is bigger than the number 95.

This gives us two rules to remember about decimals

1 To divide by 10, we move the decimal point one place to the left

2 To multiply by 10, we move the decimal point one place to the right

TURNING ANY FRACTION INTO A DECIMAL

Dividing a fraction's numerator by the denominator turns it into a decimal. This is the same as converting the denominator to the number one (rules 1 and 2). Thus

$$\frac{1}{2} = \frac{1/2}{2/2}$$

$$= \frac{10 \times 1/2}{10 \times 2/2}$$

$$= \frac{5}{10}$$

$$= 5 \times \frac{1}{10}$$

$$= 5 \times 0.1$$

$$= 0.5.$$

Write down the following fractions as decimals. All you have to do is divide the numerator by the denominator

3/4 ....

126/156 ....

100/50 ....

10/180 ....

MAKING PATTERNS
SIMPLE TO DIGEST

Looking at the table again, let's turn each fraction – that is, number of voters in each category – into a decimal. To do this, we divide the numerator by the denominator, that is the number of voters for a candidate by the total voters in the ethnic category. This would give us the following results for our table for the fraction of voters from each ethnic group supporting Trump:

White	0.568
Black	0.056
Hispanic	0.387
Other	0.418
All	0.477

YOUR TURN

Now you do it here. Write in the
decimals for each ethnic group that
supported Clinton

White ....

Black ....

Hispanic ....

Other ....

All ....

0.432, 0.944, 0.613, 0.582, 0.523

We can now see clearly what the relative levels of support were across ethnic groups. Comparing decimals, we know that more than half of white adults in the survey supported Trump, and the majorities of the other groups supported Clinton.

NOW YOU CAN MAKE PERCENTAGES

Let's return to the table. It is usually convenient to convert *decimals* into *percentages*. People are familiar with what percentages mean and can read them easily.

'Per cent' is just Latin for 'per hundred'. To convert a decimal into a percentage we multiply by 100, so we move the decimal point *two* places to the right (10 × 10). Note that a 'zero' digit counts as a place in the same way as any other number, so 0.056 becomes 5.6%, *not* 56%. Now the level of support for Trump looks like this:

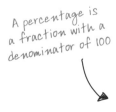

A percentage is a fraction with a denominator of 100

White	56.8%
Black	5.6%
Hispanic	38.7%
Other	41.8%
All	47.7%

Because we have expressed the numbers in the cells of the table as percentages of the totals for each *row*, we can refer to these numbers as *row percentages*.

Let's make sure you can work with numbers in a table and turn them into percentages. Look back at the table and calculate the row percentages for Clinton, and then write them down here.

. . . .

You can check whether your answers are correct by adding together for each ethnic group the percentages voting for each candidate. They should total 100. Can you see why? Each person had to choose one of the two candidates, so adding together the proportions must account for everyone!

White ....

Black ....

Hispanic ....

Other ....

All ....

We can compare things
through a table's rows
and columns

How do I read information in rows and columns?

Tables reveal many different possible comparisons. You need to be clear which one(s) you want to make.

There are four main types of comparisons in a table. The first two are simple comparisons. These are expressed by row percentages and column percentages. We look at how the fractions compare along a row or down a column of a table.

Simple comparisons

1 row percentages
2 column percentages

Comparisons of comparisons are more powerful. Instead of just comparing within a row or column of a table, we compare both things at once. This is an extremely useful technique because it gives us evidence of whether two things shown in a table are related in some way.

3 comparing column percentages along the rows
4 comparing row percentages down the columns

A CLOSER LOOK AT COLUMNS

So far the comparison we've made is of support for the candidates *within* each ethnic group. We've produced numbers that tell us, out of every hundred White or Black or Hispanic voters, how many would vote for Trump or Clinton. But we might also be interested in comparing what fraction of each candidate's support came from different ethnic groups: that is, for every hundred Trump voters, how many were White, Black, and so on. To do this we need to look at the proportion of different ethnic groups within each group of supporters, which means we are looking at fractions, decimals and percentages within each *column* of the table. To do this we calculate the fraction created by the number in each cell of the table (numerator) as a fraction of the total number for each column (denominator).

Calculate and then jot down the fraction of total support for each candidate that comes from each ethnic group. Then convert this fraction into a decimal and a percentage.

The share of Clinton's support from Whites can be expressed this way:
437/732 = 0.597 = 59.7%

Now complete your own table here with the percentage of support for each candidate that came from each ethnic group:

	Clinton	Trump
White		
Black		
Hispanic		
Other		
All	100%	100%

ANSWERS

	Clinton	Trump
White	437/732 = 0.597 = 59.7%	574/668 = 0.859 = 85.9%
Black	170/732 = 0.232 = 23.2%	10/668 = 0.015 = 1.5%
Hispanic	68/732 = 0.093 = 9.3%	43/668 = 0.064 = 6.4%
Other	57/732 = 0.078 = 7.8%	41/668 = 0.061 = 6.1%
All	732/732 = 1 = 100%	668/668 = 1 = 100%

THE OPPORTUNITIES
ARE ENDLESS...

When we have converted the fractions into decimals or percentages based on the column totals, we can add or subtract them from each other, because they all have the same denominator (rule 5). We might want to compare the proportion of each candidate's support that came from non-Whites:

Clinton: 23.2 + 9.3 + 7.8 = 40.3%.

Do you want to know the non-White support for Trump? You can calculate that here:

Trump: _____ + _____ + _____ = _____%

So what can we make of this?

Look again at the table you've just produced. It seems that more of Clinton's support came from non-Whites (40.3%) than did Trump's support (14.1%). Very few Blacks said they supported Trump.

One hundred per cent

Note that each column of percentages adds up to 100. This must be the case as we are dividing the total number in your table on p. 97 of supporters for each candidate into the four ethnic groups. In fact, if you add the totals for Trump you will find that this comes to 99.9%. This is because we have *rounded* the decimals to three digits, introducing a tiny and irrelevant loss of accuracy. We'll look at rounding in the next section.

Now you are going to produce a new version of your table, putting all the non-White ethnic groups together in one category. Work out the numbers of Black + Hispanic + Others who supported each candidate to fill in the table below and then calculate the row and column percentages.

	Clinton	Trump	
White	—	—	1011
Non-White	—	—	389
	732	668	**1400**

Your table should
look like this

	Clinton		Trump	
White	437	43.2%	574	56.8%
	59.7%		85.9%	
Non-White	295	75.8%	94	24.2%
	40.3%		14.1%	

WHAT THIS TABLE TELLS US

If you study the table you can see that there are six kinds of comparison that we could use it to make.

1   Non-White support for Clinton compared to Trump (75.8 vs 24.2)

2   White support for Clinton compared to Trump (43.2 vs 56.8)

3   The proportion of Clinton supporters who were White compared to non-White (59.7 vs 40.3)

4   The proportion of Trump supporters who were White compared to non-White (85.9 vs 14.1)

5   **White compared to non-White support for Clinton compared to Trump (43.2 vs 75.8)**

6   **The proportion of Clinton supporters who were White compared to Trump supporters (59.7 vs 85.9)**

It is worth taking some time to think about precisely what each comparison comprises, as everyday language can be rather vague in describing it. If someone talks about 'White support for Clinton', this could mean *either* the percentage of all White people who were Clinton supporters, *or* the percentage of Clinton supporters who were White – two very different things!

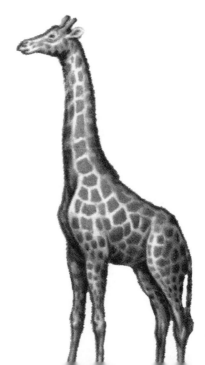

WHO'S COMPARING?

Each of these comparisons is meaningful, but the two in bold, the 'comparisons of comparisons', tell a more complete story. The bold comparison in green compares row percentages down the column of the table. The bold comparison in red compares column percentages along the row.

They tell a more complete story because they tell us if there is an association between the two things displayed in the table. Comparing row percentages down the column gives us the level of support for each candidate within ethnic groups. If these row percentages change substantially as we move down the column, then we know that candidate support varied with ethnicity. Similarly, comparing column percentages along the row tells us the proportion of each candidate's vote coming from different ethnic groups. That proportion of Trump's White vote was much higher than Clinton's.

These comparisons are also more useful because they automatically adjust for the fact that there are different numbers of people in the different categories. If we notice that only 60% of Clinton's support came from non-Whites, we cannot tell if that means that Whites were more or less likely to support her than other groups, because we don't know how big these groups are. But by comparing this column percentage along the row to the corresponding column percentage for Trump, who had 86% of his support from Whites, we can see straight away that Whites were more likely to support Trump compared to non-Whites.

CAUTION!
MULTIPLYING
PERCENTAGES

When you multiply percentages, you need to remember that they are fractions. Earlier we saw that 72% of adults in the Pew poll were White, and that 43% of them were Clinton supporters. What proportion of all people were White Clinton supporters?

Answer 72% × 43% = .72 × .43 = 3.1 which equals 31%

Now that you've thought a lot about comparing support for Clinton and Trump in the US election, let's try an exercise with numbers and data about a different issue. If you can do this, you're 100% ready to move on!

Let's start with a table. This table, based on real research, shows the number of marijuana users in a sample of men and women aged between 25 and 45:

	Women	Men	All
Use marijuana	4,086	5,621	9,707
Don't use marijuana	24,090	17,322	41,412
Total	28,176	22,943	51,119

Use what you have learnt to calculate the row and column percentages and put each in the blank tables below

Row %	Women	Men	All
Use marijuana			100
Don't use marijuana			100
Total			100

Column %	Women	Men	All
Use marijuana			
Don't use marijuana			
Total	100	100	100

your table should look
like this

Row %	Women	Men	All
Use marijuana	42.1	57.9	100
Don't use marijuana	58.2	41.8	100
Total	55.1	44.9	100

Column %	Women	Men	All
Use marijuana	14.5	24.5	19.0
Don't use marijuana	85.5	75.5	81.0
Total	100	100	100

Now you've got your results, you can answer these questions

What percentage of men used marijuana? .... %

What percentage of women used marijuana? .... %

What percentage of marijuana users
were women? .... %

What percentage of all the sample were
women marijuana users? .... %

Section

6

**Superfluous numbers
are like fog**

How do I round numbers up and down?

A

10 SEC summary

Spurious accuracy just produces clutter. Most of the time three numbers are plenty.

60 SEC summary

Long sequences of numbers mean little to anyone. When you turn some fractions into a decimal, you end up with a very long number that's difficult to read, let alone work with. So it's good to round numbers up or down to a number that uses three digits to tell the story.

'Digits' refer to the number symbols 0, 1, 2, 3 … 9 that we use to express numbers. Almost all the quantities that we need to work with can be represented accurately enough by using three digits. We can 'round off' the others to the nearest zero.

If the digits you are dropping start with 5 or higher, round the previous number up.

If the digits you are dropping start with 4 or lower, leave the previous number as it is. Just drop the numbers, no change.

A tip for making long whole numbers easier to read is to use commas. Putting commas between every three digits before the decimal point makes numbers much clearer. You can't see 1000000 without counting the zeroes, but you immediately know that 1,000,000 is 1 million.

HOW MANY DIGITS IS TOO MANY?

Think of the biggest collection of objects or people that you've ever seen where you could have counted every one. I doubt it would be a very large figure. Our brains don't cope well with large numbers.

Try imagining the difference in size between the numbers 2792466, 3117492 and 983267.

What did you do? You almost certainly focused on the first few digits in each number to get a sense of the difference. The later digits were just irrelevant. You also had to count how many digits there were. Otherwise you might have concluded that the last number was the largest, when it was actually the smallest. Now try comparing 2.8 million, 3.1 million and 0.98 million. You can see instantly which is larger, and by how much. Rounding the numbers makes them easy to see at a glance.

Most magnitudes can be expressed perfectly adequately by three digits. *Digit* is just the word used to describe the symbols like '4' or '6' that we use to represent numbers either by themselves or in combination: '46' is one number but comprises two digits; '460' or '046' or '04.6' or '.046' are three digits.

Getting rid of the remaining digits, and replacing them with zeroes if need be, makes the size of the number much easier to grasp. This is called *rounding*.

ROUNDING OFF DECIMALS

When we convert a fraction into a decimal or percentage the resulting number can sometimes be infinitely long. Thus if we express 1/3 as a decimal it comes out as 0.333333333333333...

The detail added by successive digits is usually superfluous and makes no substantive difference to the calculations we're interested in making. The extra digits just distract our attention and make things more confusing. A good rule of thumb is to use *three* digits. Often two will do. So, with that in mind, 0.333333 can be just as accurately expressed as 0.33 and is a whole lot easier to read.

To reduce the number of digits we round the number we want to use up or down depending on the value of the *first* digit that we *discard*. If that digit is 5 or greater we round up our final digit to the number above it; if it is 4 or lower we keep our final digit as it is.

Got it?

Let's go back to our Clinton and Trump voters. The proportion of Clinton voters who were White (437/732) produces the decimal 0.59699454… Round this to three digits.

The proportion of Trump voters who were Hispanic (43/668) produces the decimal 0.06437126… Round this to two digits.

Got it!

Did you get 0.597 and 0.064?

Support for Clinton: the first three digits are 596, but since the fourth digit is 9, we round the third digit up to 7 from 6. So we can write this decimal as 0.597.

Support for Trump: the fourth digit is 3 so we keep our third digit as 4. Note that we count the zero after the decimal point as a digit. So now this is 0.064.

ZEROES IN DECIMALS – PLACE IS EVERYTHING

When we are dealing with decimals, we don't need to replace the dropped digits with anything: 0.45 is the same as 0.450 or 0.450000000. Zeroes at the *end* of a decimal don't change the number.

However, zeroes *between* the decimal point and any digit *do* mean something! They put the other digits in the right place. To the *right* of the decimal point, zeroes make the number represented by the digits smaller:

0.0045 = 45/10,000

0.045 = 45/1000

0.45 = 45/100.

To the *left* of the decimal point, zeroes between the digits and the decimal point make the number represented by the digits larger:

10,000 = one × ten thousand

100 = one × one hundred

Reading lots of zeroes in large numbers is confusing. Putting commas after every third digit to the left of the decimal point makes their magnitude much clearer, allowing the reader to tell at a glance where thousands, millions and billions lie.

Round each of these numbers to three digits, writing your new number on the right-hand side.

84,940,187,685 . . . .

0.0560240414 . . . .

0.77285807811 . . . .

81,252,527 . . . .

43,490 . . . .

0.000470859 . . . .

443,000,000.1 . . . .

5927.958187 . . . .

Check your answers and if you got 8/8 you're ready to go!

84,900,000,000

0.056 ◄——— (since our third digit is a zero we can just drop it)

0.773

81,300,000

43,500

0.000471

443,000,000

5,930

Percentages and ratios help

How do I explain precise comparisons with percentages and ratios?

summary

We can put a number on
a comparison by using
fractions, ratios and
percentages.

Using numbers to make precise comparisons

When we need to make comparisons precise, we can describe them as an absolute difference or as a ratio of two numbers: the relative difference.

Ratios work in the same way as fractions. Unfortunately descriptions of ratios in English can be confusing.

The best way to make numerical descriptions of comparisons is to ensure that what you are treating as the basis (denominator) of the comparison is stated clearly at the beginning.

Percentages are often used incorrectly when making comparisons. Making sure you understand the difference between percentages and percentage points – and can clearly distinguish between them – helps keep descriptions clear.

HOW TO PUT A NUMBER ON A COMPARISON

In Section 5 we made a 'comparison of comparisons' to look at the relationship between ethnicity and support for Trump and Clinton.

While 75.8% of non-Whites supported Clinton, only 43.2% of Whites did so. Non-Whites were more likely to support Clinton.

The next step is to say something about *how much* greater Clinton's appeal was to non-White voters.

There are two ways we could describe this difference. These are absolute difference and relative difference. Both are correct ways of describing the difference between the support for Clinton and Trump, but they tell us different things. Let's look closer.

CALCULATING ABSOLUTE AND RELATIVE DIFFERENCES

We can subtract 43.2% from 75.8% to get 32.6%. This is the *absolute* difference between Clinton's share of the White and non-White vote.

But we could also *divide* 75.8% by 43.2% to get 175%. This is the relative difference between the two shares. It can sometimes be expressed as '75% higher' since the value 100% would mean 'the same level'.

THE PERIL OF PERCENTAGES

The difficulty is how we write it down in a sentence. If we simply write 'Clinton's share was X% higher among non-Whites', it is not clear whether we are referring to the *relative* or *absolute* difference. If we are referring to the relative difference, it is not clear whether X% means X or 100 + X! In newspapers you will find the same wording being used for all three of these formulations, even though they each produce very different results.

COUNTING
WITH APPLES

The confusion in language comes from not being precise about describing comparisons. Say I have four apples and someone gives me another two.

I could say

I have two more apples!
The absolute difference between four and six: 6 – 4 = 2

I have 1.5 times as many apples!
The relative difference between four and six: 6/4 = 1.5

My number of apples has increased by half!
The absolute difference,
as a proportion of the initial amount: 2/4 = 1/2

All of these are correct, but they're explaining what has happened to the change in my fruit bowl in a different way. You will also find each of these expressed as percentages.

WORD IT MORE CLEARLY

To make this clearer you can use the term 'percentage points' when describing absolute difference. This makes it clear that you are describing scores on a scale that goes from 0 to 100. Thus Clinton's support share among non-Whites was 32.6 percentage points higher than among Whites.

You can use the language of multiples rather than percentages to describe relative differences, using decimals. Thus Clinton's vote share was *1.75 times greater* among non-Whites than among Whites.

RATIOS

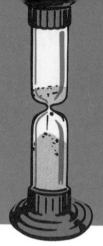

The number 1.75 is an example of a *ratio*. It tells us how much bigger or smaller one number is than another. Ratios are just another form of fraction, but they commonly exceed the value of 1.

We calculate ratios in exactly the same way as fractions. We divide the number we want to compare (the numerator) by the original number (the denominator).

Just like fractions, we can arrange things so that the denominator is a convenient number like 100. Ratios like these are often referred to as index numbers, especially when making comparisons over time. Let's look at the value of vinyl records to get to grips with this a bit better.

THE VALUE
OF VINYL

Here's a table that shows the cost of vinyl LP records in
the United States from 1965 to 2005:

Year	Cost in $ at current prices	Average per capita weekly income in current $	% weekly average income	Consumer price index	Cost in 2015 $
1965	3	49	6.12	16	19
1970	4	69	5.80	20	20
1975	6	103	5.83	27	22
1980	7	164	4.27	41	17
1985	8	245	3.27	55	15
1990	10	325	3.08	67	15
1995	12	394	3.05	79	15
2000	13	492	2.64	89	15
2005	15	597	2.51	100	15
2015	24	801	3.00	122	20

Let's read this table. It shows some data about the price of LPs in the United States over the last 50 years. The contents of the table we examined earlier, comparing support for Clinton and Trump, were based on one sample of people. This table is different. Each column contains information from a different source, but each row of the table presents this data for a single year.

Based on what you've learned so far about how to read numbers in a table, check which of these statements is true:

1 LPs cost twice as much in current \$
   in 1985 compared to 1970   True / False

2 Average income in current \$ has more than
   doubled between 1995 and 2015   True / False

3 An average earner in 1975 could buy
   20 LPs with their week's pay   True / False

1   True

2   True

3   False They could buy 100 ÷ 5.83 = 17 LPs

ARE THINGS GETTING MORE EXPENSIVE?

Of course, prices change over time because of inflation. To measure this, economists use a *price index* that measures the changing cost of a representative basket of goods over time. (Doing this is harder than it sounds. There were no mobile phones, CDs or personal computers in 1965, while few people in 2005 were buying typewriters!) Thus the fifth column in the table shows that a basket of goods costing $16 in 1965 would have cost $122 in 2015. This is a way of showing us that, yes, the prices of things do get gradually more expensive over time.

THE PRICE INDEX

This index is a series of ratios that we can use to move between current prices and 'real' prices that stay the same over time. We can use rule 4, along with these index numbers, to move between current prices and 'real' dollars, and get a better sense of historical change.

We multiply the price in current dollars by the ratio of the price index for the two years we are interested in.

HOW MUCH IS AN LP IN 2015 $ THAT COST $4 IN 1970?

$$\text{Value in 2015 \$} = \text{1970 price} \times \frac{\text{2015 index}}{\text{1970 index}}$$

$$= \$4 \times \frac{122}{20}$$

$$= \$24.40.$$

The table shows that while the price of an LP has steadily increased from about $3 to $25, once we take account of inflation its real cost in 2015 has gone back to what it was in the 1960s or early 1970s. However, this price represents about one-half of the proportion of average weekly income now compared to what it did then.

#LittleQuickFix

Reading the table, put a tick next to the statements that you think are _true_, and a cross next to the ones you think are _false_

1   Mean weekly personal income in current dollars reached 16 times its 1965 level in 2015   ☐

2   The relative change in the consumer price index between 2005 and 2015 was 22%   ☐

3   The absolute change in the consumer price index (2005 = 100) was +22%   ☐

4   Current prices more than doubled in the 1970s   ☐

5   LPs cost five times more in 2005 compared to 2015   ☐

6   As a proportion of mean income, LPs were at their cheapest in 2005   ☐

7   Between 1965 and 1975 the price of LPs doubled
Between 1975 and 1995 it doubled again
Between 1995 and 2015 it doubled again   ☐

ANSWERS

1 ✓

2 ✓

3 ✓

4 ✗

5 ✗

6 ✓

7 ✓

Work through this checklist to ensure
you have mastered all you need to know
in working with numbers. If you can say
'yes' to all six, you're done!

☐ Manipulate fractions: multiply, divide, add and subtract them

☐ Move between fractions, decimals and percentages

☐ Read and interpret row and column percentages in tables correctly

HOW TO KNOW
YOU
ARE
DONE

- [ ] Recognize ratios and use them in calculations

- [ ] Understand the distinction between absolute and relative differences

- [ ] Recognize different types of tables

Glossary

Common denominator A denominator that takes the same value for two different fractions.

Decimal A fraction expressed using the base 10 numbering system as tenths, hundredths, thousandths, etc.

Decimal point The point, written like a full stop or period, that marks the division between the column for units and the column for tenths in a number that is written as a decimal.

Denominator The bottom line in a fraction which gives the number of times the number one is to be divided up when evaluating the fraction.

Digit A symbol used to represent a number. '2', '25', '2.5', '.52', '52' are all numbers. The 2 and the 5 are digits used to represent them.

Divisor A number by which another number is to be divided.

Fraction A whole number divided by another whole number, where the result is not itself a whole number.

Index number Index numbers are numbers expressed as a percentage of a base figure, usually 100.

Numerator The top line in a fraction which gives how many units of the denominator fraction there are.

Percentage A fraction with 100 as the denominator.

Placeholder The digit 0 in any number, inserted to keep other digits in the correct place.

Proportion Another name for a fraction.

Ratio The comparison of the size of two numbers.

Rounding Treatment of the final digit of a decimal number, when digits to the right are dropped.

Spurious accuracy Digits superfluous to those needed to understand the magnitude of a number.

Table cell The number at each intersection of the rows and columns of a table.

Table column Each vertical line of numbers in a table.

Table row Each horizontal line of numbers in a table.

Whole number A number that describes any quantity that is *not* a fraction.